PROTECTING OUR RIVERS AND LAKES

Text: Rosa Costa-Pau
Illustrations: Elvira Soriano
            Jordi Segú

La Defensa de los Rios y los Lagos © Copyright
Parramón Ediciones, S. A. Published by
Parramón Ediciones, S. A., Barcelona, Spain.

Protecting Our Rivers and Lakes copyright ©
1994 by Chelsea House Publishers, a division
of Main Line Book Co. All rights reserved.

1 3 5 7 9 8 6 4 2

Defensa de los rios y los lagos. English.
   Protecting our rivers and lakes.
      p. cm.—(The Junior library of ecology)
      Translation of: La Defensa de los rios y los
lagos.
   Includes index.
   ISBN 0-7910-2105-X
   1. Water—Pollution—Juvenile literature. 2.
Water quality management—Juvenile
literature. [1. Water—Pollution. 2. Pollution. 3.
Water supply. 4. Water quality management.
5. Environmental protection.] I. Chelsea House
Publishers. II. Title. III. Series.
TD422.D44 1994   93-19878
363.73'94—dc20   CIP
                                              AC

Contents

PROTECTING OUR RIVERS AND LAKES

961614

CHELSEA HOUSE PUBLISHERS

New York • Philadelphia

Water from Nature

THE WATER CYCLE

We can use water over and over again. This is because it goes through a continuing natural cycle. Water from the earth's surface escapes into the air through evaporation. When the water vapor in the air reaches a certain concentration, it condenses and returns to earth in the form of precipitation.

LAKES, STREAMS, AND RIVERS

If we could observe a hilly or mountainous territory from the air, we would see that its landscape consists of a kind of mosaic of different pieces, all arranged so that the water circulates toward the sea. Water flows down the slopes through forests and over mountains where passageways have been cut over time. Brooks and streams run into one another, finally making a river that grows increasingly larger.

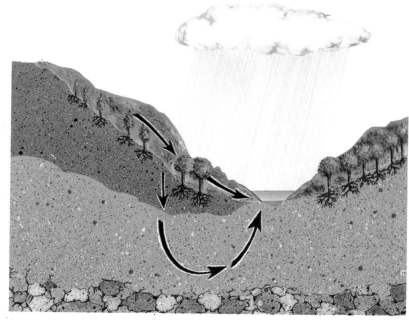

▲
Precipitation is absorbed by forests and soils, but eventually most of the water finds its way back to the sea.

Flood waters are often captured in reservoirs and irrigation channels for use in agriculture.

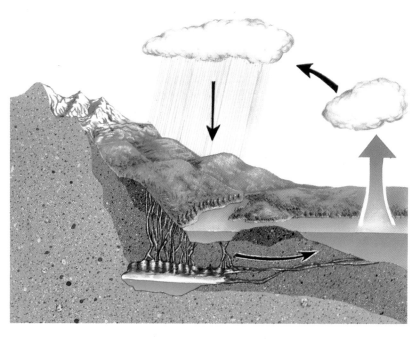

Some water filters through the ground until it reaches an impermeable layer, creating subterranean reservoirs and streams. Water falling from the atmosphere in different forms returns to the sea from which it evaporated.

When the water reaches a barrier or a depression it may be retained, causing lakes or ponds to form.

The hydrographic basin, or water basin, is composed of a system of streams, lakes, and ponds carved out of mountainous regions. This area is the source of the water that feeds the river.

Sometimes the river is not large enough to carry away all the rainwater flowing into it from its smaller tributaries. This can cause floods and devastation to the communities along the river banks.

But people have learned how to take advantage of flooding in some places. In ancient Egypt, the flooding produced by the river Nile was called the Gift of the Nile. It was given this name because the river deposits large amounts of fertile, loamy soil that produces rich and varied harvests.

Rivers transform barren regions into rich agricultural land and places suitable for human habitation.

The Hydrographic Basin

THE FLOW OF RIVERS

The river carries more or less water depending on the season and whether it is a dry, normal, or wet year.

The flow of a river is the quantity of water it carries past a given point in a certain time. To calculate the flow of a river we multiply its width at the point being measured by its depth and by the speed of the water. The result is expressed in cubic meters per second.

THE VEGETATION OF THE RIVER BASIN

The amount and type of vegetation covering a river basin affects the composition of the river water.

If rainwater is filtered through the tops of trees, it hits the ground with less force and runs off slowly without carrying away as much material as it would if it fell directly onto the ground. When the river basin is bare of vegetation, it is exposed to constant erosion.

The landscape of a hydrographic basin is made up of forests, fields, rocks, rivers, and lakes. In fact, these are different ecosystems that are closely related to each other, so that a change in one may modify the functioning or the structure of the others.

Rivers are also an important means of transport.

Dams are built to regulate the river's flow in seasons of intense rain. The hydraulic power stations built into them are also an important source of energy.

River water is used in agriculture, but the overuse of fertilizers and pesticides may cause the water returning to the river to be polluted.

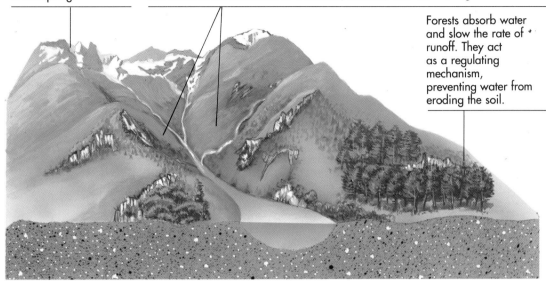

Glaciers provide river basins with meltwater in the spring.

The upper part of a river basin is formed by the steep slopes of the mountains. This leads to the formation of waterfalls, torrents, and fast-moving streams.

Forests absorb water and slow the rate of runoff. They act as a regulating mechanism, preventing water from eroding the soil.

The basin of a river includes all of the territory whose waters flow into it. The illustration shows the upper stretch of a river. The altitude, slope, and the lay of the land all determine how the river will flow—fast and relatively straight or slow and meandering.

HUMAN ACTIVITIES IN THE RIVER BASIN

As it runs down to the sea, river water is used to good advantage in many ways.

Some of humankind's activities are not harmful to the river environment. Other actions, however, such as changing the course of a river or cutting down forests to create fields, can present a serious danger to the ecosystem.

These actions not only change the landscape of the river basin, they also cause serious changes that affect the growth and development of many living organisms.

Along the middle section of a river's course there is often an intense concentration of industry producing pollution.

Throughout history, rivers have played a fundamental role in the development of humankind, supplying water and fish and providing a means of transportation. Today, however, people's actions can cause serious changes in the river ecosystem.

The River: An Ecosystem

FOOD RELATIONSHIPS

In a food chain or food network there is always an organism called the producer. This is a green plant that captures sunlight and uses its energy to transform minerals into food, which is then consumed by the other animals in the food chain of the ecosystem. The food is consumed first by herbivorous animals and is then passed on to other *consumer* organisms.

FOOD PRODUCTION

When the tops of trees block out the sunlight, the *photosynthesizing* plants do not have sufficient energy to produce food.

When this occurs, organisms living in the river depend for their food on organic matter: leaves, branches, and seeds coming from neighboring ecosystems.

Many insects live together among fallen leaves and appear to feed off them; in fact, they feed off the bacteria and fungi growing on the surface of the leaves.

Insects masticate this organic material, grinding it into very small pieces. These insects, called masticators, play an essential role in the decomposition of matter into fine particles, which are deposited on the riverbed or remain suspended in the water.

Other insects, called collectors, use a special type of mouth apparatus to feed on the particles deposited at the bottom of the river, while the particles that are in suspension become the food of insects called filter-feeders.

PREDATORS

Predators are the animals in an ecosystem that feed on other animals. Their survival depends on the health of the producer organisms.

Insects are an important element in the animal life found near rivers. Many insects feed on the bacteria and fungi that flourish on the surface of leaves that have fallen into the water.

Human development, home construction, and the clearing of land destroy the habitat of producer organisms and the creatures who depend on them, making river ecosystems barren of life.

Plankton is the nutritional base for other organisms in the river.

Carp are a common species in rivers. They generally feed on worms, molluscs, small crustaceous creatures, and insect larvae.

When the slope of the land diminishes and the speed of the water decreases, vegetation can gain a foothold on the banks of the river.

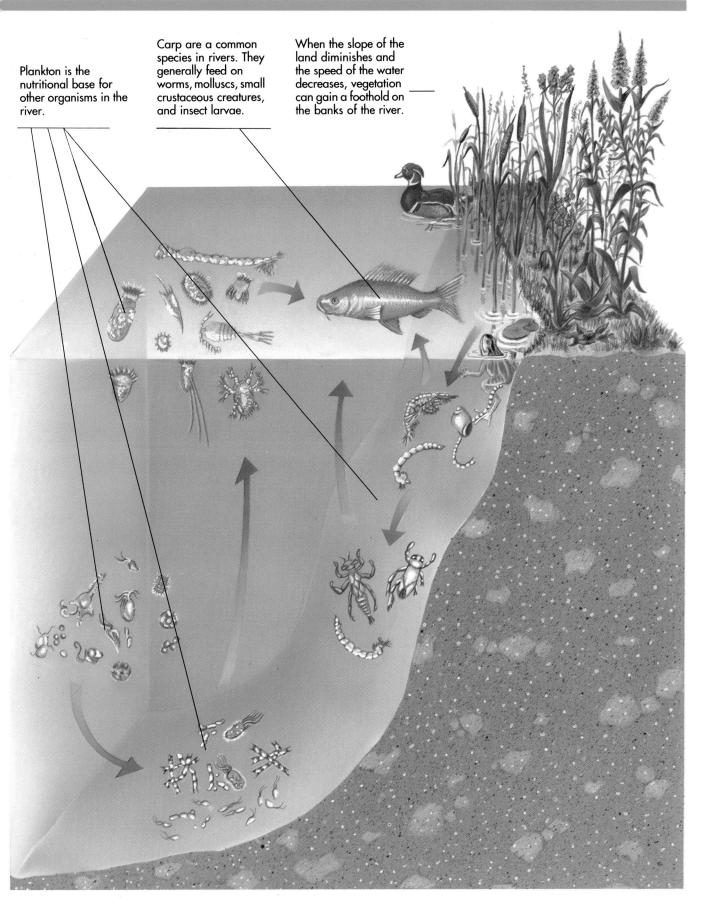

Running Water

WATER AS AN AGENT OF TRANSPORT

River water is constantly in movement, forming currents that take the water toward the sea. These currents cause the water to come into contact with vegetation, rocks, and soil, often dissolving mineral substances such as salt, lime, or clay. These materials, like the leaves and branches of trees, are transported by the river, giving the water a particular composition and set of properties.

The so-called upper stretch of the river generally has a pronounced slope that causes the water to flow quickly, producing intense erosion of the banks and riverbed.

In the middle stretch, the water still runs at a considerable speed, although the slope of the land is much more gentle.

In the lower stretch, on nearly flat land, the river does not follow a straight course. It forms loops called meanders. The word meander means a wandering, sinuous course.

ORGANISMS CARRIED ALONG BY THE CURRENTS

In order to assure the survival of their offspring in the river water, female insects lay a large number of eggs. When the adult insects emerge from the larval stage, flying or sometimes crawling, they move against the current and lay their eggs at a higher level.

In a river, therefore, because of the current, organisms found in the lower stretches exert a constant pressure on those that live upstream.

The communities of living organisms found in different areas of a river cannot be studied separately one from another.

▼

10

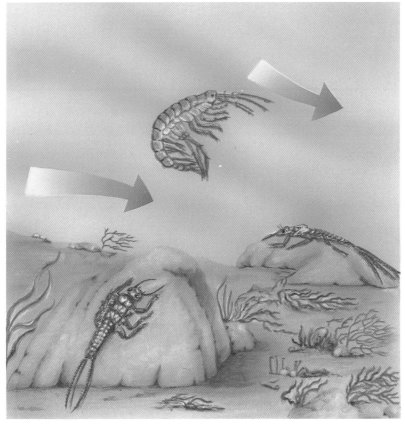

▲
The current of a river drags living organisms downstream, especially the larvae of aquatic insects.

RIVER COMMUNITIES

The slope of the river, the speed of the water, the material deposited along the riverbed, the temperature of the water, and the vegetation found on the banks are all factors that directly or indirectly favor the development of one type of organism over another, thereby forming different ecosystems in different areas along the river.

Along the upper stretch of a river, where the temperature is not usually higher than 60°F, algae form green patches on rocks. Various types of worms and insect larvae colonize all parts of the river.

As the slope diminishes, the water speed decreases, the temperature rises, and the vegetation on the river bank flourishes.

When the river runs into the sea, the speed of the current decreases and the matter it is transporting falls out as sediment. Animal species here are quite varied; the species found most frequently is the carp.

River Fish

THE MOVEMENT OF FISH

In order to better survive in the water, fish respond to different stimuli. The response to light, for example, is very important for fish. Some respond negatively, that is, they avoid light and remain at the bottom of the river. The fish called miller's-thumb lays its eggs beneath rocks and submerged tree trunks, and the males watch over them until the eggs are hatched.

In general, the reaction of fish to certain stimuli help them to find food, defend themselves against predators, or simply orient themselves when they need to travel from one place to another in the river.

FISH IN THE UPPER STRETCHES OF THE RIVER

Just as with other organisms, the distribution of fish throughout the river basin is conditioned by factors such as temperature, the amount of available oxygen, the ease of finding food, and the slope of the riverbed.

Fish have elongated bodies that offer little resistance to the current. They also have strong muscular systems that enable them to swim upstream or to remain motionless in the water. This is useful for capturing prey floating downstream on the surface of the river.

The predatory fish that inhabit the upper stretches of rivers frequently move down to the middle or lower stretches.

FISH IN THE LOWER STRETCHES OF THE RIVER

The lower stretches of rivers are particularly vulnerable to the effects of

The slope of the riverbed is one of the prime factors affecting fish in most mountain rivers, because they must be able to overcome the pull of the current to move upstream to breed.

climatic changes. During the summer, when the water level drops, the fish gather in groups in certain areas. They generally remain in holes where the water is calm to wait for the first autumn rains.

Carp and catfish are typical species of the lower stretches of rivers. Their flat bodies and large scales help carp and other freshwater fish to move easily.

The construction of a reservoir at a point along the river where there once were rapids produces changes in the current and in the life that the river will support. ▼

◀ *The eel swims downstream and crosses large expanses of ocean to find food and then returns to its spawning place. The eel can adapt to different conditions in sea and river water.*

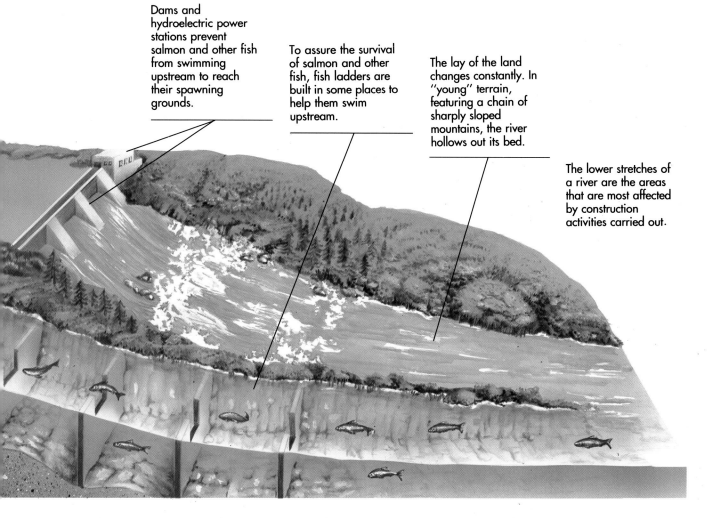

Dams and hydroelectric power stations prevent salmon and other fish from swimming upstream to reach their spawning grounds.

To assure the survival of salmon and other fish, fish ladders are built in some places to help them swim upstream.

The lay of the land changes constantly. In "young" terrain, featuring a chain of sharply sloped mountains, the river hollows out its bed.

The lower stretches of a river are the areas that are most affected by construction activities carried out.

Rivers and Man

WATER ENERGY

Since ancient times, people have searched for ways to make work easier by looking for new sources of energy.

Running water has enough energy to move objects, including heavy tree trunks, downstream. Water can also turn the vanes of a waterwheel.

In the parts of rivers that had torrents and rapids, people soon discovered that they could take advantage of the force of the waterfalls. The invention of the waterwheel made it possible to use this force to do work. It was first used to turn mills. This is why the first industries grew up beside fast-running rivers.

Building dams on the waterfalls made it possible for the water to fall from a greater height so that the hydraulic force was also greater. This force could be used to move more complicated machines, such as turbines driving electric generators.

When electricity was discovered and came into use, it was no longer necessary to locate industries beside waterfalls since electrical energy could be transported from one place to another.

IRRIGATION WATER

Because of the differing amounts of precipitation during different seasons of the year, water often has to be stored up during rainy seasons.

Many areas of the earth require more water than is supplied by rain, so it is necessary to artificially irrigate the land by channeling river water.

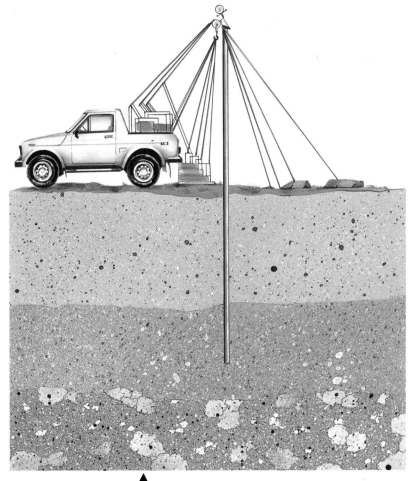

▲

Wells are dug until they reach the level of porous rock where underground water has formed an aquifer.

It has been possible to cultivate many desert regions thanks to artificial irrigation systems. The dam built across the Nile, the world's second longest river, has changed the life of this river and has led to the creation of an extensive area of land suitable for cultivation. ▶

UNDERGROUND WATER

Subterranean water is taken from wells dug into the ground at different depths.

The greatest amount of water is consumed near the coast, where cities and factories are found. For this reason, more wells are found in coastal areas.

When groundwater is used continually, its level drops and seawater enters the wells. Particularly in the summer when water consumption is highest, drinking water in a coastal city may be salty.

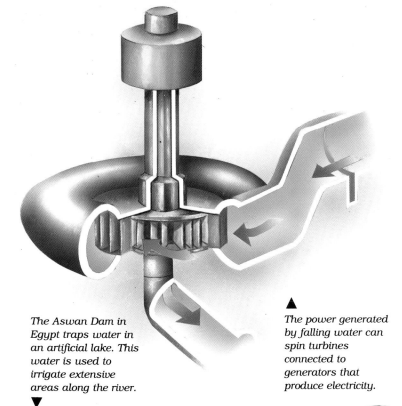

The Aswan Dam in Egypt traps water in an artificial lake. This water is used to irrigate extensive areas along the river. ▼

▲

The power generated by falling water can spin turbines connected to generators that produce electricity.

From Source to Sea

THE COURSE OF THE RIVER

Through ravines and valleys the river wends its way down toward the lowlands until it flows out into the sea. Along its course the water may flow over obstacles that do not erode easily, causing it to change its speed. This is how rapids, waterfalls, and cataracts are formed.

When the water encounters depressions or hollows in the land, it flows very slowly, causing the formation of ponds, lagoons, and lakes.

LAKES

Water accumulates in lakes because there is usually more water entering than flowing out.

A lake, despite its apparent stillness, is a place where a large number of organisms live. Here, plants and animals find suitable conditions for growth and reproduction. Birds, fish, insects, frogs, microorganisms, and various plant species make up a feeding cycle.

The character of a lake as a freshwater ecosystem is defined by specific temperature conditions and levels of light, oxygen, and carbon dioxide, as well as nutrient levels and the way the water moves.

PLANTS

The microscopic plants that make up the phytoplankton, together with the wide variety of higher plant species growing on the banks and the bed of the lake, assure the production of food through photosynthesis.

The water flea, a species belonging to the zooplankton, is a tiny insect that filters water to feed itself on phytoplankton. Lake plants bend easily to cope with water currents.

Insects that live in the lake have evolved to take advantage of the conditions of this ecosystem.

Insects play a very important role in the flow of energy and food within the lake.

Temperature, light, oxygen, carbon dioxide levels, and the movement of the water are the factors that define the characteristics of the lake as a freshwater ecosystem.

In deep lakes where the bed is not very soluble, being made of rocks such as granite or slate, and in areas where there is no agriculture, the production of nutrients is at a low level.

In lakes where the bed is made up of soluble rocks, the water is full of nutrients, particularly if fertilizers run off into the lake from nearby cultivated land.

Lakes with a high nutrient content usually have green water. These lakes are called eutrophic lakes.

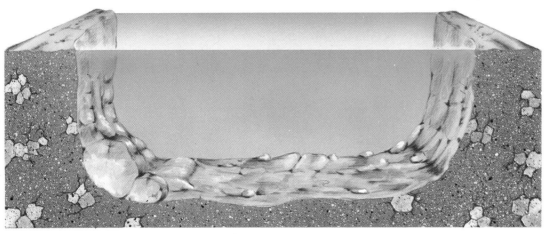

Eutrophication means an increase in nutrient levels, but this is actually a form of pollution caused by excessively high levels of organic matter, nitrogen, and phosphorus in the water. Algae thrive in this environment, choking off other plant and animal species.

The animal and plant species that populate a lake make up a community of organisms known as a biocenosis.

The lesser duckweed, which has a single tiny root, lives by floating on the water. The water lily, fixed to the bottom of the lake, has a special stem with an oxygen reservoir for breathing. The trout feeds on the vegetation near the banks. The frog and several aquatic birds share the bank of the lake with other nearby land creatures.

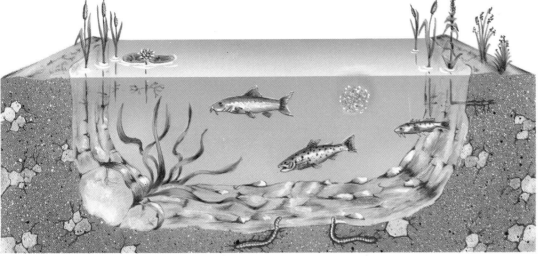

The Pollution of Rivers

WATER FOR LIFE

Just like other living creatures, human beings need water to grow and survive. The water we consume throughout the day usually comes from a river. But this water must be pure and clean so that it is safe for drinking. When the water is not pure or clean, we say it is contaminated.

The World Health Organization (WHO) considers water to be polluted or contaminated when it has lost the properties it has in its natural state, that is, when its composition has been altered. For example, when the proportion of oxygen in the river water decreases, this may result in the asphyxiation and death of fish and other organisms.

Uncontrolled fishing, the introduction of foreign species of fish that endanger the survival of the local species, the drying out of lagoons, the construction of dams and canals, and increases in temperature due to the influx of warm water from power plants are all factors that directly or indirectly alter the composition of the river water and reduce the possibilities for survival of the plant and animal life it supports.

SOURCES OF CONTAMINATION

Although the pollution of a river may be accidental or due to natural causes, it is most often caused by man-made contaminants in the sewage water from cities, the chemicals used in agriculture, or the by-products of industrial activity.

Sewage water coming from cities contains human waste, detergents, and cleaning products. The water that comes from cultivated fields and range lands usually carries excrement as well as fertilizers and insecticides used in agriculture.

Under normal conditions, bacteria maintain the level of oxygen needed for animal respiration. However, if the input of organic matter is greater than the purifying capacity of the bacteria, the oxygen level decreases and life is endangered.

When pollution is caused not only by organic matter but also by industrial waste, the contaminating molecules may be absorbed by the inhabitants of the river and passed through the food chain to many different organisms.

▼

EFFECTS OF POLLUTION

Normally rivers can purify their own waters and reestablish their natural characteristics.

There are bacteria living in river water that slowly decompose the organic matter coming from the remains of living creatures and plants. These bacteria reach the river either directly or through the sewage water from urban areas.

To carry out this decomposition, the bacteria need to consume oxygen, which they obtain from the water itself. These bacteria are called *aerobes*.

◄

The prime source of river pollution is water coming from industrial activity: paper mills, petroleum refineries, chemical industries, nuclear reactors, and oil- or coal-fired power plants.

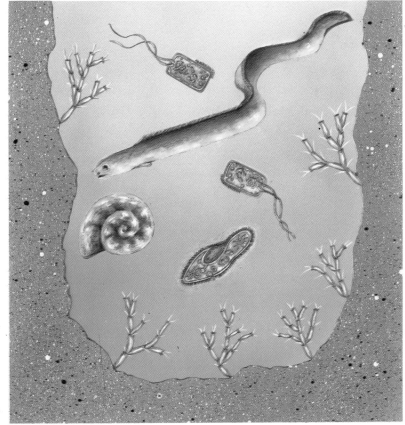

The Contamination Cycle

CONTAMINATION OF WATER

The problem of river pollution not only affects the life forms that inhabit its waters, but is a growing source of concern to the industries that need water of a certain quality to maintain production.

The industry that pollutes river water may therefore be one of its first victims because of the circulation of contaminants.

Organic matter, chemical substances such as insecticides, and radioactive substances are just some of the contaminants that, once they are in the river, go from one organism to another and from community to community, circulating through the food chain.

INSECTICIDES

DDT was one of the first insecticides used to combat insect pests. Since it is now known that this substance is harmful to other forms of life as well, other pesticides are used instead in ever increasing quantities.

One of the most significant ecological disasters caused by the uncontrolled use of insecticides occurred in the Coto de Doñana in Spain during the summer of 1973. This incident led to the poisoning of 40,000 birds in this sanctuary.

RADIOACTIVITY

Large amounts of water are needed to cool nuclear reactors. Once used, this water is returned to the river. The aquatic plants and many microorganisms quickly absorb the radioactivity, and this produces a weakening of the ecosystem.

Radioactive substances enter the river and circulate in the same way as other contaminants. The river's radioactivity is passed on to people through the fish caught in the river. ▶

Heat is a factor that ▶ influences the rhythm of biological activity and reproduction for many living beings. When the water temperature rises, some organisms may increase to the detriment of others.

The increasing use of river water by industry produces a rise in the water temperature.

The growth of only some species causes the ecosystem of the river to lose some of its diversity so that its structure changes. The ecosystem becomes simplified and functions with greater difficulty.

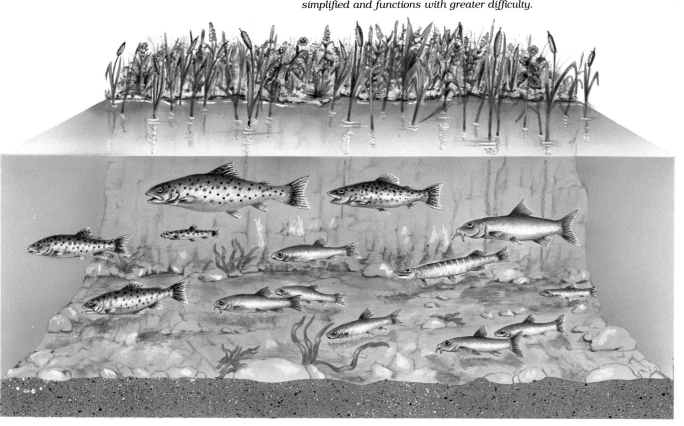

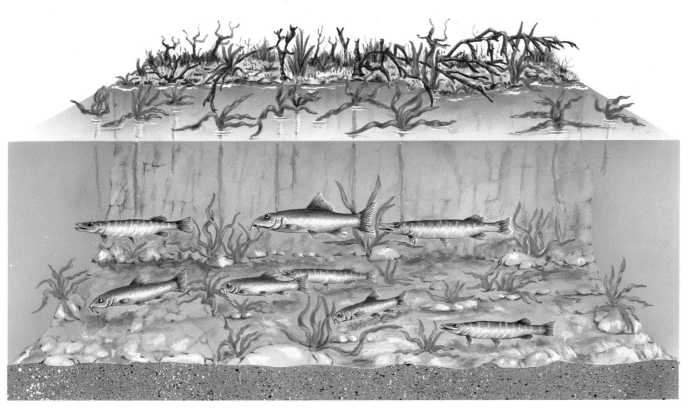

Characteristics of River Water

THE FUNCTION OF WATER

The water that circulates around the planet earth may be compared to a giant still, that is, an apparatus for evaporation, circulation, and condensation. This still also works like a large machine that distributes heat uniformly over the surface of the planet.

If the earth had no water cycle, like the moon, the sun's rays striking different parts of its surface would produce extremely high temperatures at the equator and extremely cold regions farther away from it. Life would then be impossible on earth.

Water absorbs heat as it evaporates and gives it up when it condenses. Water vapor, like river water, carries heat when it drifts across the continents heading toward the sea. In this way, a variety of ecosystems are created, from crystalline springs and mountain lakes, containing only small amounts of dissolved substances, to lakes that can be saltier than the sea itself.

THE COMPOSITION OF RIVER WATER

By simply looking, it is hard to tell the difference between rainwater and seawater. But if we taste the water, we are able to easily recognize seawater by its salty taste.

Seawater is salty because it contains dissolved salts. Rainwater, on the other hand, is a pure substance.

River water, like seawater, contains dissolved salts. The mineral salts in the river come from the rocks and the earth of the river basin. The most important component is calcium bicarbonate, which is found in very small concentrations.

The quality of water is very important to human life since some health problems, such as dental decay and loss of bone calcium, can be aggravated by constantly drinking water that does not contain the necessary mineral salts.

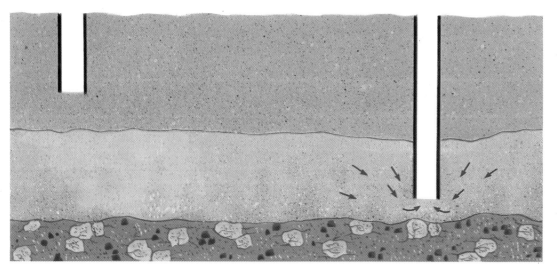

◀

When it falls on permeable terrain, water penetrates into the ground until it reaches the level called the water table. Sometimes an aquifer is formed. Aquifers are regions of permeable rocks that can store water in their open spaces. In the aquifers, water circulates from one place to another. Wells are drilled to bring up the water stored in an aquifer.

WATER FOR HUMAN CONSUMPTION

For centuries, the cities suffered from great epidemics because of the water people drank. Dirty water was not separated from water used for drinking and cooking. The people did not know about the existence of microscopic life and the connection between illness and certain microorganisms.

When the dirty water infiltrated the ground, it contaminated the wells and springs and caused epidemics.

When it was observed that dirty river water could be a vehicle for the microbes that caused diseases, pipes were constructed to separate water for consumption from dirty water, which was conducted through a separate sewage system.

Humans can directly use only a small amount of the water in the hydrosphere. Purifying seawater is only done on a small scale, and using water from ice floes has not yet been attempted.

To conserve water resources it is essential to maintain sufficient vegetation on the surface of the continents.

Continental freshwater consists of all the water flowing in rivers and streams, groundwater, and lake water. This is the water that people can use.
▼

▼

Reservoirs and Springs

WATER STORAGE

Dams and reservoirs, besides producing electricity, also regulate the flow of river water and store it up so that it is available when needed for consumption and irrigation.

To create a reservoir, a dam is constructed across a river and the water level rises until a vast lake is formed. A sluice gate in the dam lets out the water that is not needed. In times of abundant rainfall, the river water accumulates. The reservoir receives little or no river water during periods of drought.

In times of drought, farmers use reservoir water to irrigate their fields. The water passes from this artificial lake to irrigation channels and from the channels to the fields.

DRINKABLE WATER

Generally, water for human consumption is pumped from a river or reservoir to a purification plant. From this plant it is transported to tanks or water towers situated at a higher level than the places where the water is consumed so that it flows down easily.

After the purification process, water is used for human consumption, where it becomes contaminated once again.

▶ *Underground springs also produce a popular product known as mineral water. These springs are generally found in areas away from sources of contamination, but they are tested periodically for impurities.*

In times of drought, the lake receives very little water, sometimes none. The water that accumulates during the rainy season is used little by little, and the water level goes down steadily.

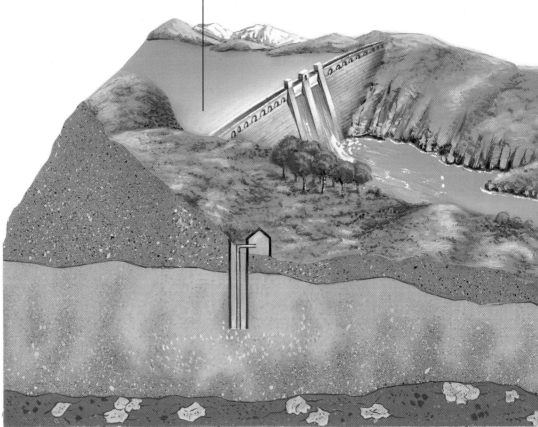

▶ *In a water treatment plant, the composition of the water from the reservoir is analyzed and the water is treated to make it drinkable.*

There is groundwater almost everywhere. In rainy regions, groundwater is close to the surface. When the nonporous rock layer is close to the surface, water is also near.

A spring is formed when groundwater comes out of the earth's surface.

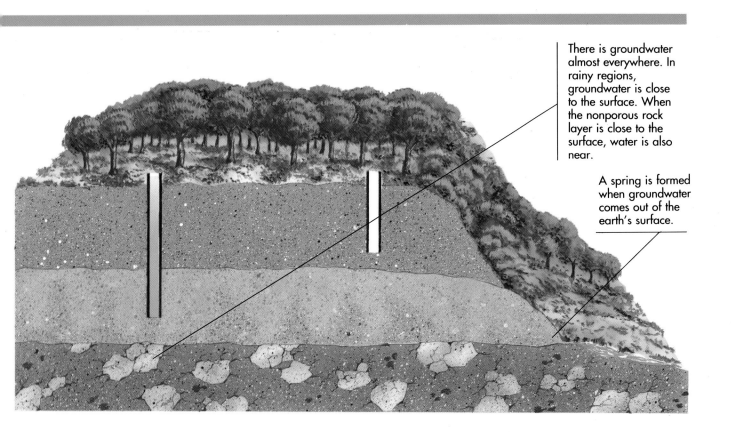

Sometimes when houses in the city are at a higher level than local water tanks, pumps are used to make the water reach the highest floors of the buildings.

In a city, it is not only necessary to supply sufficient drinking water, it is also necessary to provide for the treatment and removal of sewage before the water is returned to the river or is dumped into the sea.

▼

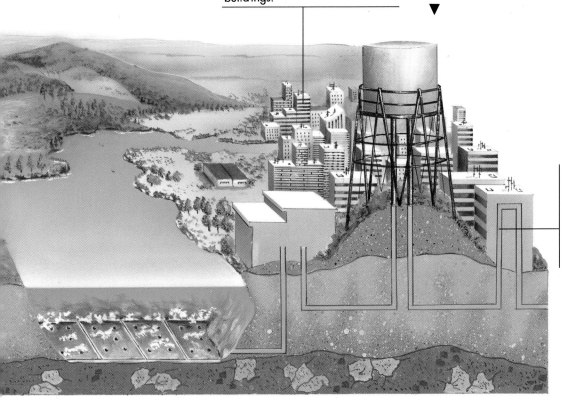

The characteristic taste and smell of tap water is produced by chlorine, which is added to kill microorganisms that could infect the population.

The Treatment of Sewage Water

REMOVING CONTAMINANTS

Sewage water from cities eventually flows into a river, a lake, or the sea. This water may carry many pollutants and toxic substances, so it must be purified.

Water is treated and purified in special plants using different techniques and procedures, depending on the type and quantity of contaminants in the sewage.

UNDERWATER PIPELINES

An *underwater pipeline* is a long conduit that carries sewage water to the sea far from the shore. Under certain conditions a pipeline can be a good solution, since the self-purifying capacity of the sea may be able to recycle the contaminants if the water is widely dispersed and does not contain non-degradable toxic substances.

STAGES OF PURIFICATION

One stage of the purification process is carried out using screens or filters that retain solid residue. The sand used in the screen holds back the larger particles suspended in the water. This is the mechanical phase of purification.

The biological phase involves eliminating the organic matter found in sewage water. To do this, conditions are created that are favorable to the growth of microorganisms that decompose organic matter by feeding on it. A large amount of oxygen is needed, and this is introduced by means of air injected into a ventilation tank.

Fast-moving water, called white water when it causes turbulence and rapids, has a strong erosive effect that causes the formation of mountain valleys.

As it carves its way through solid rock, water dissolves and transports large quantities of minerals.

Humans often contaminate the water more intensely and more quickly than nature is able to purify it. This is why in many regions it is necessary to purify the water needed for human consumption by artificial means.

▼

Water is an indispensable element for the survival of human beings.

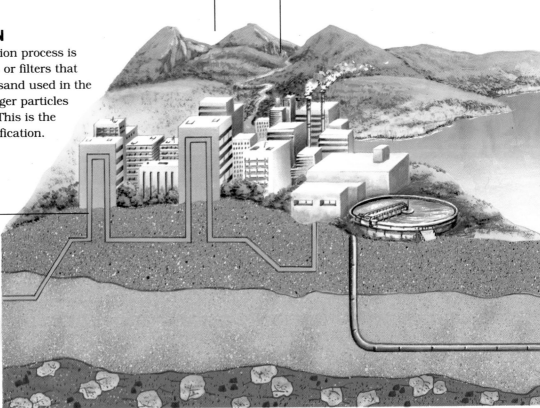

The location of freshwater reservoirs does not always coincide with the location of large urban and industrial centers. The shortage of water makes it necessary to transport water from other places along canals or even by modifying the course of a river.

Organisms that resist the contamination or pollution of water are what we call indicators of the level of contamination.

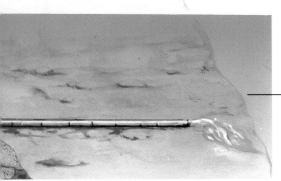

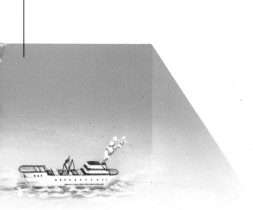

On the continental shelf, algae and other plant species thrive. All of these are food producers, so the contaminating substances that enter the sea are a serious risk to marine life.

By means of chemical procedures, some contaminants in the water are made to coagulate, that is, to form easily removed viscous lumps. In this way, they can be eliminated using sand filters and screens.

SPECIAL WATER TREATMENT

Appearance and taste are not enough for us to be able to judge whether water is suitable for consumption. Many pathogenic microorganisms are invisible to the naked eye and have no telltale taste. For this reason, water must be properly disinfected.

Chlorination is one way of ensuring that the water is free of pathogenic microbes. Ozone treatment and ultraviolet radiation are also currently used to disinfect water.

In order to remove certain types of molecules found in contaminated water, it is filtered through absorbent substances such as carbon.

At the end of the entire process, the sewage water is once again returned to nature. Sewage water is, therefore, removed from the natural cycle for a certain period. After it has been used and treated, it is channeled and transported to a lake, a river, or the sea.

Things You Can Do Yourself

A HYDRAULIC TURBINE

Building this simple turbine will help you to understand the principles behind the operation of hydraulic turbines. These turbines are used in hydroelectric plants to transform mechanical energy into electrical energy.

MATERIALS

A CORK

A PIECE OF WIRE

A PAIR OF SCISSORS

A PLASTIC BOTTLE

Cut the bottle as shown in the drawing. Make holes in both sides of the bottle and in the bottom.

With the plastic left over from the bottle, cut 6 small pieces. These will be the vanes of the turbine.

Punch a hole through the cork and pass a piece of wire through the hole.

Make slots in the cork and put pieces of plastic into these slots.

Place your turbine beneath the water tap so that the water falls on the plastic vanes. Notice that before running out through the hole at the bottom of the bottle, the water spins the vanes of the turbine. This motion may be transformed into other types of energy.

SEDIMENTATION AND TRANSPORT OF MATERIALS

You can reproduce the mechanisms of transport and sedimentation in the river in this simple experiment. The lightest materials remain in suspension in the water and are carried along by the current. Heavier materials are deposited, or sedimented, along the river bed.

A PLASTIC BOTTLE

SAND

GRAVEL

SMALL STONES

Fill the bottle three quarters full with water.

Place the bottle on a table and wait a few moments while the water becomes still. Notice that some material is deposited on the bottom of the bottle, forming layers, while other materials remain in suspension in the water.

Put sand, gravel, and small stones into the bottle.

Cork the bottle and shake it for a few seconds.

REPRODUCING THE WATER CYCLE

You can simulate nature's water cycle at home. All of the elements of the cycle will be present: water vapor, clouds, and rain.

A PLASTIC BAG

ICE CUBES

A BOWL CONTAINING WATER

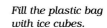

AN EMPTY BOWL

Ask an adult to fill one of the bowls with hot water.

Fill the plastic bag with ice cubes.

Hold the plastic bag over the bowl of water. The water vapor condenses on the lower part of the bag. The ice cubes begin to melt and "rain" also begins to fall into the other bowl that you are using to collect the water.

Words To Remember

Aerobe An organism that needs free oxygen from the air in order to live.

Anaerobe An organism that does not require any free oxygen, such as certain bacteria that live in the river water.

Autopurification The gradual elimination of an excess of organic matter from a system through the activities of the microorganisms living in that system.

Basin An area irrigated by a single river or watercourse and its network of tributaries. Basins that do not drain into the sea by way of a river, and whose waters have no outlet, are called closed basins.

Channel An open waterway where water that is destined for irrigation and other uses flows.

Chlorination Adding a certain amount of chlorine to water destined for domestic use in order to disinfect it.

Consumers All animal organisms that cannot produce food. These are called herbivores if they eat plants and carnivores if they eat meat.

Eutrophication An increase in the quantity of nutrients in a lake. This may be produced by natural mechanisms or by human activity, and in some cases it can be a form of pollution.

Photosynthesizers Plant organisms containing chlorophyll that are able to carry out photosynthesis, that is, food production or the production of organic matter.

Soluble The characteristic of dissolving easily. A rock is soluble if its mineral components dissolve in water.

Underwater pipeline A duct or pipe built to deposit sewage water into a lake or the sea at some distance from the shore to facilitate its dispersion. This method is only advisable for small towns near the coast.

Vegetation cover The degree to which a surface is covered by various types of plants. The greater the density of vegetation, including grass, bush, and tree cover, the greater the coverage of the land.

Index